WE TURNED BACK TO SEE WHERE WE CAME FROM

SNAPSHOTS, VIGNETTES, AND STORIES
BY THE STUDENTS OF
GREATER EGLESTON HIGH SCHOOL

AN 826 BOSTON PUBLICATION

BOOK PRINTING BY
WESTCAN PRINTING GROUP,
WINNIPEG, CANADA

COVER DESIGN: ERICA LEE
INTERIOR DESIGN: ERICA LEE AND ROBERT DAVIES
PHOTO EDITING: JOHN PAUL DOGUIN
COPYEDITING: CARA BAYLES

ISBN-10: 1-934750-16-6
ISBN-13: 978-1-934750-16-2

826 BOSTON
3035 WASHINGTON STREET
ROXBURY, MA 02119

617.442.5400
WWW.826BOSTON.ORG

826 BOSTON IS A
NON-PROFIT ORGANIZATION
DEDICATED TO TEACHING
CREATIVE AND EXPOSITORY
WRITING TO STUDENTS
AGES 6 TO 18, AND TO
HELPING TEACHERS INSPIRE
THEIR STUDENTS TO WRITE.

This book was published with generous support
from the Ludcke Foundation
and the Boston Cultural Council

This program is supported in part by a grant from
the Boston Cultural Council, a local agency which is funded by
the Massachusetts Cultural Council and administered
by the Mayor's Office of Arts, Tourism and Special Events.

TABLE OF CONTENTS

ESCAPING THE FIRES OF LIFE

LA MAGIA DE LA VIDA

I'VE BECOME ART

AND THREE MORE

PHOTO BY AIXA LARA

FOREWORD

We all have a 'coming to America' story. Whether you were brought to this country as a baby immigrant like me or whether you were born in South Boston, we all have a story of how we got to this 'here.'

When I was almost two years old, my mom traveled from Mexico by plane with me and my two older brothers and sister. We were on our way to meet my dad, who had already moved to Chicago. We would live there first and then make our way to Brookline. But on this day, we had to pass the immigration checkpoint at the Dallas airport before we made our connection to Chicago.

The super-tall Texan immigration agent with the super-thick accent towered over my five-foot-tall mom who also had a very thick accent—a Mexican one. The agent inspected all of our green cards, looked my mom and the four kids up and down and apparently sideways, and then he bellowed out an order: "You are welcome to come into this country..." he said, his drawl lingering. But then he looked at me. "Everyone but that little baby. I can see a rash on her skin and she will have to stay here in quarantine."

My mom didn't feel very powerful as she was being looked down upon and ordered to leave her baby behind in a new country. But she reached deep down inside and found her power in her gut and puffed up all the five feetness of her tiny body as tall as she could. And then, as if a volcano erupted inside of her, she found her voice. She *trusted* her voice. And she looked up at that agent and said, "No sir! I weel not leeve my daughter here with chu. She is coming with me. She eez not sick! And I weel not leeve without her. Do you HEAR ME? I weel not leeve her here!"

The tall Texan suddenly felt very small next to my mother's big and powerful voice. "Yes, ma'am," he said. "You can all come in. I am sorry!"

Ever since I heard my coming to America story, I have used it as an inspiration to find my own gut, my own power, my own voice when I feel powerless. If mom could do that almost 50 years ago—tiny and accented and in a new country—I can surely find my own voice when I feel tiny and unheard and powerless.

Sometimes, when you feel invisible, it's easy to feel voiceless. And when you feel voiceless, then you learn how to not use your voice. And when you don't use your voice, you don't hear yourself. And when you don't hear yourself, it's hard to trust who you are.

But with my coming to America story, my mom showed me that words are power. Your voice is your instrument—whether you speak (with an accent or not), write, sing or shout. It can be a literal sound or it can be your voice on a piece of paper or a computer screen. But it is yours. And it comes from *your* gut. So maybe you should trust it.

I remember thinking because I was a bit different, no one else saw the world like I did. I was a Mexican immigrant kid growing up on the south side of Chicago. There weren't a lot of other kids like me. I did feel different. I felt small. At times I felt voiceless. I thought I was the only student who felt powerless and not part of the 'real America.' I know now that wasn't the case. I know now that many kids felt different but we just didn't talk about this. Ever.

The young writers in this book are not of my generation. I read what they are writing and I know they can see and feel and touch how the world is changing all around them. It gives them a new identity, a new way to use their power. They are taking charge; they are making words and ideas their own. They are owning their power.

The trick is to know how to trust that inner voice. That writer's voice. That poet's voice. That journalist's voice. That screenwriter's voice. The unique voice each one of us has. It's the voice that comes from the same place my mom found her own voice that day. From in your gut. And when you realize that your gut is a truly powerful place, then you can begin to trust it. And when you trust that inner voice as a voice of power, you let it take you where the story needs to go. Even if it isn't pretty. That is the kind of honesty I see in the writing of these student authors. Visceral. Honest. Gut powerful and gut wrenching. Powerful words. Because in fact, they trust that they do have power. As writers. As Bostonians. And as Americans.

But, writers, let me warn you. Sometimes people will just look at you and say: "WHAT IS THAT? You can't write." Don't worry. They said it to Mark Twain and Langston Hughes and Sandra Cisneros. But if you can hear the sound, if you can feel the rhythm, if you are speaking, writing, singing in your own voice with your own sound, if you can feel it in your gut, you're on your way. Own the voice and own the power, young writers. The rest of the world is waiting to see what you powerful people have to say.

Maria Hinojosa
SENIOR CORRESPONDENT FOR *NOW* ON PBS AND
AUTHOR OF *CREWS* AND *RAISING RAUL*

INTRODUCTION

G ive young adults digital cameras, allow them the freedom to capture, reflect on, and write about images that matter to them, and they will become inspired to write. The images and essays in this outstanding book represent the students whose voices eloquently describe how their lives have been impacted by the people and events they have encountered. These encounters come in the form of joy, sadness, and the range of emotions in between.

As this year-long writing project progressed, the staff and I could see the growth of our students' writing skills and overall character. The more they wrote, the higher their confidence levels became; the higher their level of confidence, the more risks they were willing to take. A new cycle was beginning to emerge in our students. The opportunity to work in partnership with 826 Boston tutors throughout the school year resulted in a year of growth through self-reflection and discovery.

We Turned Back to See Where We Came From is a wonderful achievement for our young authors and a tribute to a successful partnership between Greater Egleston High School and 826 Boston. Teachers and 826 Boston staff and volunteers mentored our students through a journey that required students to show compassion,

resilience, and desire to be regarded as achievers. I am immensely proud of what each student author has accomplished. I know after reading this book, you too will share in our celebration and the realization of a dream.

Julie Coles
HEADMASTER, GREATER EGLESTON HIGH SCHOOL

LOVE

IS THE RIGHT WORD FOR THIS

Outside Laundromat

SHANESE SIMMONS, AGE 19

She washes the laundry and hangs it outside to dry in the cool winter breeze. She cleans all day while her husband is at work and her kids are at school.

She makes her bed and lies down to rest her feet. She is tired, and that's why she's not on the porch checking to see if her laundry is dry. She's thinking about her worries. Or perhaps she has fallen asleep, and dreams about escaping the fires of life.

PHOTO BY SHANESE SIMMONS

PHOTO BY SHONDA WILLIAMS

My Grandmother

SHONDA WILLIAMS, AGE 17

She's the one who prepares
  the soul food when I'm hungry,

She's the one who gives me medicine
  when my stomach aches.

She's the one who turns my
  fiery-eyed frown into a bright, beaming smile.

She's the one who wipes thick,
  watery tears away from my sad eyes.

She's the one who whacks the strict branch
  on my little behind when I fail to mind her.

She's the one who helps me to be joyful.

She's the one who shows me that when
the darkness comes, things will always get better.

She's my struggle.

She's my heart.

She's my passion.

She's the one who reminds me to read
my Bible when my mind is all over the place.

She's the one who lets me struggle
and learn from my mistakes.

She makes me realize that love is
always going to be here.

My grandmother's the rock that keeps this family
together. She's the golden smile when I glow.

PHOTO BY SHINEEKQUA WALKER

My Baby Sister

SHINEEKQUA WALKER, AGE 18

She might look like a little angel now, but don't let the smile fool you; left by herself, she tries to pull her schemes over on my mother, just like I did. Like they say, "Don't judge a book by its cover." She's a handful. Once she painted my room's walls bright red with her popsicle, then laughed like the little devil she is. She cut up my favorite pants and took my shirt as if it was hers and wore it to school to show off to her classmates. I guess that's a little sister's job: to annoy her big sister 'til she turns red. But I have a feeling that her fun days of making my life so crazy and upside down are over. Now that we have a younger baby sister, she will go through what I did. Good luck, baby sis. You're going to need it.

PHOTO BY AIXA LARA

Gone

JAVIER "JACOB" CASADO, AGE 18

DECEMBER 6, 2009

Ma was braiding my hair.

Phone rang.

Thought it was an invitation to family dinner.

"I don't want to tell you,

Pupie passed away."

You're out of my life but still in my memory.

Looking at your picture on the wall,

thinking, *Why?*

Walking up to you, about to shake your hand.

Forgetting they took you from us.

Just waiting for you to wake up and say,

"What's good, Jacob?"
Waiting for you to tell a joke or two.
Looking at you lying there,
tears falling out of my eyes.

NOVEMBER 28, 2009
Shaking your hand.
Last time laughing at you.
"Yo, Blick, give me my money."
Looking at you walk out that door.
Last time I saw you.
"Aight then, bro."

MARCH 4, 2010

Trusting no one.

I still can't believe it,

looking at your picture every day,

not wanting to think of it,

but I still see you.

Thoughts of you make me cold,

thoughts of you make me want to do good.

Battle of Stop & Shop

SHINEEKQUA WALKER, AGE 18

Running and screaming all around the store, they are finally still for a moment. "Everybody say, 'Cheese!'" someone shouts, and before you know it, zoom! They take off again, one hitting the east side of the store as the others take the west and north sides. And this is what my mother calls "Family Day Out." Yeah, right. This is more like "Let's Get on Our Big Sister's Nerves Day."

Their favorite game is hide and seek. Why do I always have to be the seeker? Running up one aisle after them, I hear them giggle and laugh. My brother runs straight into a stack of balls, face first, as his partner in crime keeps running. All I can think is, *Yes! One down, two to go.* I bring him back to where we first started, as he kicks and screams, grabbing and knocking down all the potato chips.

PHOTO BY SHINEEKQUA WALKER

Not too far away, I end up running into the second one. There's one more left to catch, but I have to be really careful: the oldest girl is so sneaky that we call her "the little fox." As I creep down the aisle looking for Ms. Sneaky, I hear my mother scream from aisle two, "Five minutes until we leave. Hurry up!"

Then the next thing I know, a hundred balls come flying at me all at once. *Dang! She's good.* But luckily she tripped over one of the balls that she threw. Back to Mommy we go, as the bag boy pushes our food into the bag. "It's time to go. Did y'all have a good time?" Mom asks.

As smoke starts to blow out of my head, I think about my warm bed. I consider how I can lock everybody out of my room and relax. With a big smile on, I say, "Okay, Mommy. It's time to go home."

Summers

JOSHUA SANTOS, AGE 19

I am thirteen years old, young and energetic, feeling the hot summer day on my back. A baseball game is the first thing on my mind this morning as I get ready to head outside. My friends are outside with me, and my sister strolls in the backyard to join us. As we pick teams for the infield and outfield, we notice that the number of people watching us multiplies and the small playground turns into a baseball field. It is comforting to know that my sister is there playing and enjoying herself as much as I do with my friends.

On hot days, I go to the pool and take a dip or two in the water. I look at all the pretty girls in the pool and my friends dare me to talk to a lifeguard and ask her out on a date. It is working—until she notices I am younger than I appear. I am nervous and smiling at the same time because she is so beautiful. My friends are laughing as I get rejected and I turn away to dive in again. I yell, "Crap!" underwater. I always have a blast with my friends no matter what activities are planned or how embarrassing they turn out to be.

PHOTO BY SHANESE SIMMONS

Man! I wish I could go back to the days when everything was perfect. I didn't have worries in life because I was just too young and new for the world's troubles. All I had to worry about was being a companion to my sister, a good friend who never said no to playing outside, and a loyal son to my mother.

Thanks to This Car

ASHLEY BRITO, AGE 17

Mississippi, 1930. Those were the tough times—we had no money and our car was broken. The car was a luxury. We could hear it from far away when my dad was coming home. I was five years old, my mom was nineteen, and my dad was twenty-two. The economy was bad, and finding a job was even worse. My dad worked while my mom cooked and took care of me. My mom worked around the house, and I tried to help her by dusting and picking up shoes and toys from the floor.

My dad's only option was to drive our car as a taxi. But when the car broke, he couldn't even do that because we had no money to fix the car. So my parents decided to switch positions. He would take care of me while she went to work. My mom went out every morning looking for a job until she found one as a seamstress in a clothing store called Escalante. She loved the work she did. Her dresses were so beautiful that within a few months, she was already doing very well.

After a year, she opened her own shop and called it Adam's Family Dress Shop. I liked to watch my mom sew there. I thought her dresses were beautiful and made every woman who wore one look unique. Even the wealthy women of the town bought them.

So, I thank this car. We never gave up, and we keep this broken car to remember where we came from.

THE DEAD END

GINA PEGUERO, AGE 20

When I walk down this street, I get goose bumps wondering what could happen. I don't really know the people who live here. I am walking in a horror movie. I see lonely, mysterious people, isolated from everything else. I see shadows of people moving the curtains to peek outside and see what is going on. A black cat wanders around, following me as I pass by.

I wouldn't like to live like an old lady who has always been trapped in her home, not knowing what's going on around her. I'm afraid of the suspicious man in a suit with a disheveled button-down shirt, getting out of his car. He forgot to shave for the past three days. He's got these dead, black eyes that make me nervous and uncomfortable on my walk home. He looks at little girls in a way that makes me want to turn around and run. I fear these things when I see, or even pass by, a dead-end street.

PHOTO BY GINA PEGUERO

DEEP SLEEP

ALFRED PHILLIPS, AGE 17

I am in a black-out deep sleep, when I feel something crawling on me. I think I am home and my mom is trying to wake me up, so at first, I ignore it. Then I feel it again. I feel cold, so I get up to close the window. When I finally pop up and look around, I am confused. I am not home at all. I don't know where I am. I have a million little spiders crawling on me, so I take my shirt off. I keep trying to think and remember how I got here.

I am trapped in this room, wishing to be free. Every time someone walks by, I bang on the door yelling,

"Help! Someone rescue me!" The room is dark. The only light comes from the window. It is empty and cold. Sometimes I look at people passing by and it seems like I'm invisible as they keep walking. I don't know how long I can last inside this room.

NOT AS COMFORTABLE AS I LOOK

SHAWN WEEKS, AGE 18

Yellow walls with a portrait of Brenda in her beautiful, fluffy wedding dress and Jay, with a Colgate smile, in his sharp snow-white tuxedo. I loved sitting on the brown linoleum floor that squeaked when pressure was applied to it. I felt like this was home forever.

Everywhere I looked used to be clean. Now it's leaves, trash, and cardboard boxes. The temperature used to be just

PHOTO BY SHONDA WILLIAMS

right, but now I'm outside and it's windy and cold. Are these leaves ever going to be picked up? Can somebody fix this wall behind me? Four walls that had nice pictures on them once surrounded me, with flowers in vases that made me smile from ear to ear—not different-colored graffiti writing and leftover food all over the place.

Times can get tough, but I tend to stick it out. I relax and make the best of life while watching the days go by through mailman weather. I just wish I could be as comfortable as I used to be.

I wake up to a loud beeping noise and a spoiled fish smell. I don't know what is going on. Two smelly guys grab and lift me. They carry me towards the beeping and fish smell like I am nothing. Next thing I know, I am swimming in fish guts, dirty papers, and all types of junk. Then the walls start coming together. My frame is going to break! These walls are hurting me. Someone stop this!

BOMBING

RAHIYM MERVIN, AGE 17

pray cans, paint markers, Sharpies, and blank stickers: the supplies of a graffiti artist are like explosives. Molotow spray paint costs about eight bucks a can. Paint markers cost about four dollars each. Sharpies, depending on which ones you get, can cost between three and six dollars per pack, but the Sharpie Magnums are sold individually and cost about

four dollars. You can get the blank stickers free from your local post office. An artist loves his supplies.

Making graffiti is called bombing or tagging. It is a form of art. Tagging can be dangerous, adrenalin-pumping action.

When bombing, you have to rid yourself of fear to be great. You have to be a risk-taker and go all out and leave your mark in a place that's hard to clean. Look for places that are high and surfaces that spray paint can really cling to.

Trying not to get caught or have his supplies confiscated are the two main goals of a bomber. An artist can always get more supplies but they're expensive and you have to be eighteen or older to buy them. Relying on someone else to get supplies for you can be a waste of time, because they can let you down when you really need them.

Bombing is illegal. The police call it vandalism and malicious destruction of property. When an artist is caught, the consequences depend on how ruthless the artist has been.

The more tags you have around the city, the more property you've destroyed. If you're a beginner artist, your explosives are just confiscated by the cops and you have to do community service. If you're ruthless and tagging all over the city, the maximum consequence is two years in jail.

CELL

CHNIA WILLIAMS, AGE 17

There's no bathroom or bed. All I do is sit here and wait. There are no windows or lights. I start feeling lonely and scared. I'm alone. I don't know what time it is or how long I've been in here. Bars on windows, moldy ceilings, broken tiles on the floor, rusted old broken lockers, dusty floors, weird smells, mouse traps, and metal doors. I haven't eaten or drunk anything in hours or maybe even days. I start feeling sick. I'm getting weaker and weaker as time passes by. My nails start to grow long and curl like snails. There is a rotten stench and it smells lifeless, like a dead rodent on the street. This cell has been here for years; no one cares that I'm in here. They don't even care enough to clean our cells. They just throw us in here and forget.

PHOTO BY CHNIA WILLIAMS

PHOTO BY GINA PEGUERO

THE FIELD

GINA PEGUERO, AGE 20

hen I was fifteen, Franklin Field was full of kids playing football games and people drinking, listening to loud music, and parking their cars everywhere.

Gang members from Franklin Hill and Franklin Field projects used to shoot each other over whose projects were better. I would hear the ambulance and police cars. I could sense the fear in innocent people. Girls got raped and killed and people got robbed day and night.

I remember this one kid named Jonathan who went to the same middle school as me. A quiet, Dominican kid, short and skinny with brown, innocent eyes. He would always go to school, do his work, and mind his own business. Then he got to high school and he started hanging around with bad people who influenced him to join gangs, fight, smoke, and drink. It was disappointing to me.

One day he cat-called a girl who was with her boyfriend. When the girl's boyfriend heard him shouting at her, he got mad and went up to Jonathan's face. That's when they started fighting. All of a sudden, I saw the sixteen-year-old take out a gun and shoot Jonathan right in the stomach. It was a shocking moment. There were people yelling, crying, and running for their lives. When I got a little bit closer I saw a river of blood pouring down his body.

Franklin Field is different now. The Boston Housing Authority has moved most of the gang members who used to live there. Some of the gang members were sentenced to jail for years. Meanwhile, the neighbors in Franklin Field are trying to make it better. In the future, I see myself walking around, smelling barbeque, hearing bachata, and watching the kids play basketball and baseball like they used to do.

HER PRESENCE

CORENNE SKEEN, AGE 18

ll of a sudden I hear someone running through the woods. Leaves are crumbling and a girl is screaming for help. She lost the charm bracelet that her mother gave her before she passed away. It represents that the girl's mother is still in her presence.

She begins to look for it. She tries to retrace her footprints, but she gets lost looking for it. Fortunately, she finds her way out. From this moment on, she knows she is never going to see the bracelet again. She feels discouraged as she walks away with her head down.

Everyone has lost something in the past, whether it is something small and replaceable or something very important. Whatever it is, it's gone and never coming back.

PHOTO BY MARQUES BELL

PHOTO BY RAHIYM MERVIN

NIGHT OF AN ARTIST

RAHIYM MERVIN, AGE 17

It's a little past nine on a snowy school night. He can't sleep so he goes for a walk. He grabs his jacket and leaves. He decides to do a throw-up while he's out, so he grabs a can of yellow spray paint.

He walks to a school yard and spots a nicely painted red brick wall. He walks over to the wall, looks at it, then thinks to himself that yellow and red are a good combination of colors. He graffitis on walls for the adrenalin-pumping feeling. He likes the way his heart beats fast.

He looks around to see who's near. He sees no one. Then he looks up at the school building, and sees no surveillance cameras. He pulls out the can. His heart beats fast, but he's relaxed. His tag is not a word or a name, it is just letters that he likes. Five minutes later, he's done. He tosses the can, snaps a picture, and walks away, leaving his mark.

PHOTO BY RAHIYM MERVIN

LA MAGIA DE LA VIDA

HYDRANT MEMORY

JESSENIA NUÑEZ, AGE 18

Birds fly in the hot summer sky. Water rolls down the pavement from the open fire hydrant, watering down my friends playing in the street. I hear the doorbell and I quickly strap on my Velcro sneakers, the ones with flashing lights on the bottom. I run down the stairs, excited to play double-dutch. On my way to the sidewalk I come across my mother. She is on her knees pulling up leaves from around her idol, which was made by human hands. She makes it look so pretty. As the night falls, winter enters. The days start to grow colder and the trees grow barer. Slowly but surely, snow begins to cover it up. The statue gets covered in snow. Months go by and it begins to melt. Out of nowhere, I see a vine wrapped around the fence and the flowers start to bloom.

PHOTO BY ALFRED PHILLIPS

PHOTO BY MARQUES BELL

BOMBING THE SYSTEM

WILFRED GONZALEZ, AGE 18

People walk through our communities looking at graffiti, calling it vandalism. I call it art. From my point of view, the graffiti fills the city with color. This tag has some nice colors and detailed letters that show an arm and a face. When you focus on the second letter, you notice a sleeve with a fist on top. The last letter is a face with an X for eyes and big teeth with black paint dripping out. Both the second and last letters are filled with white so they stand out more. The second letter shows a form of strength. This graffiti piece is well done, with clean curves and an outline.

You will always find graffiti on top of other graffiti. When a tagger takes up good wall space and doesn't do a good job, the next graffer will come by and tag it up, claiming that spot with his art. The only way a writer can go over another writer is if he has more skill as an artist. If someone has a "whack piece" and is taking up good space, then you can expect a good tagger to throw his art on top. The writer with less skills and experience is more likely to get tagged over and to be shown no respect.

If I were to put something on this wall, I would write, "Artist, Not Vandal." Graff taggers write because it is something they feel proud of. When they are out in the streets, they see their own art work on the side of a big building and they know people are wondering who did it, and how they got up there. The meaning of the pieces is mostly unknown to the public, but the writer knows their true meaning. As a graff writer, you put your thoughts and emotions into one picture, and it creates a strong connection with you. Graffiti is public art that makes the community.

WHAT'S INSIDE

INDIGO WILKERSON, AGE 18

When I finally decided to go to church at age six, I felt a bit shy, as if I didn't belong. Pleasant Hill Baptist Church was big on the outside, and there were stairs on the inside that made it feel huge. I visited with my grandmother, who wore a silky shirt and little skirt, and my grandfather, who wore a suit. They took me inside and introduced me to the pastor.

As I looked around, I saw a familiar face from around my neighborhood, which made me feel better about being the only kid in church. This took away some of the shyness that I had built up inside of me. After sitting down for a while, my grandparents took me downstairs to the lower level of the church where the other kids were. I felt relieved to know that there were more kids going to church than I'd thought. I finally made my way over to them and started playing games. Before I knew it, church was over.

PHOTO BY LEYLA PIZARRO

I realized that you can't always listen to what other people say about something; sometimes you have to find things out for yourself. I once thought church was a bad thing, but it actually turned out to be good. Looks can be deceiving. This might look like a regular bottle, but you never know what message is inside until you pick it up and find out.

MOSES

KELMAR BRADFORD, AGE 18

pring 1955, a year after the murder of Emmett Till. A white pastor named Moses, who lived in Mississippi, decided to leave the South with his wife and kids to start a new life in Massachusetts. He heard racism wasn't as strong as in the southern states. Moses was angered by the injustices of Till's trial. He didn't want his kids to grow up in a place where segregation and murdering blacks were acceptable. He packed up everything he wanted to keep, including his dog, favorite church clothes, his Bible, and some of the kids' toys. He planned to send for the rest of his belongings once he was in Boston.

As he drove north up the East Coast, the old Ford went *erh, erh, erh.* His young kids slept in the backseat. His wife slept on the passenger side. He drove, just thinking. He thought about his kids and hoped they would like Boston. He wanted them to grow up without the hatred and ways of the South. He hoped they would make something good of them-selves. Maybe become teachers or doctors and help all kinds of people, including black people. He hoped they would understand the decision he made to leave Mississippi.

PHOTO BY SHANESE SIMMONS

Spring 2010: Moses' granddaughter is about to get married to a black man, a doctor and a good man. He loves Moses' granddaughter. Moses III, the bride's brother, refuses to attend the wedding. The other brothers and cousins beg him to attend, to make the wedding a real family reunion. Moses speaks to the grandson who has his name and tells him the reasons he moved his white family to the north. He once moved his whole life away from racism, and now sees it again in his own grandson's face.

Moses tries his hardest to convince his grandson, and sees a change in his grandson's face. He has decided to go to the wedding. Moses smiles.

THE PRINCESS IN THE GHETTO

AIMEE PEREZ, AGE 17

I n fairy tales, you always hear that the princess lives in the highest room, in the tallest tower. But I'm just a regular teenage girl trapped in the highest room of the crappiest building in the ghetto.

Around the same time every day, when the sun goes down, I sit at my window looking down at the view and people who stroll by. I always see the same people: a group of kids walking down the street, smiling and laughing. Oh, how I wish I were with them. Freedom is all I ask for, or possibly an extra long braid that my friends could climb up to keep me company.

How boring this view is from my window. Nothing but other project buildings with vines covering the windows and bricks missing, so all I see is the white cement that keeps them together.

If only my building was an expensive hotel with room service and catering. A banana split with hot fudge and a cherry on top would really make me happy, but the vending machine downstairs only dispenses chips and candy. This is where I ended up, trapped in an old building with nothing to look at but a sparkling, new, white picture frame with a picture of a laughing family, instead of a window.

PHOTO BY SHAKAYLA VENABLE

AS WE STROLLED

SHAKAYLA VENABLE, AGE 17

A s I walk through the park holding hands with the one I love, we stop and think, *Should we carve our initials into this tree? Do we really want people to know?* He picks up a light, oval-shaped rock that's near the tree and begins to carve my initials. As I watch, I notice his manly hands. The tree is old and strong, but he makes this look easy. When it's my turn to etch his initials, I struggle because I'm not as strong. So he gently grabs my hand and guides it as we carve his initials together.

When we finish, we stop and look into each other's eyes and say, "I love you." As we turn back to the tree, I take a snapshot in my mind so I can remember this moment forever. I think to myself, *Did this really happen? Did we really do this?* Now the world will see that we are here to stay. Love is the right word for this.

UP THERE

MICHAYE WEST, AGE 19

I live in Dorchester, and this is the view from the top of my house. I can see the other buildings surrounding my house, a lot of trees, and a little bit of downtown Boston.

The view from inside the John Hancock Building, on the top floor, is totally different. When you look down, everything is so little. The trees look like grass and the streets look like little paths that cut through it. There's so much more of Boston you can see.

My favorite view of Boston is the view of the Charles River from the John Hancock Building. You can see how the river breaks up the land and the multiple bridges that connect the land. The Red Line train crosses a bridge over the Charles River and right behind the bridge is the Liberty Hotel, which used to be the Charles Street Jail.

It's beautiful at night. If you go to the top floor of the John Hancock and stand at the front, you can see UMass Boston, which looks as if it's floating on the Boston harbor that circles around it.

PHOTO BY LEYLA PIZARRO

REST. IN. PEACE.

JESSICA FELICIANO, AGE 17

Rest In Peace. What do you do when you hear that? I cry, because when someone I am close to dies, it hurts. It's like a part of me is gone.

My best friend told me that a girl named Paola was shot. A boy killed her in her own house. At first, I thought it was not true, but when I saw her picture, my heartbeat stopped. She was

PHOTO BY JESSICA FELICIANO

four months pregnant and only 18 years old. I had known her since middle school. We would always say, "Hi," and talk.

The last day I saw Paola I walked to her house. She asked me if I was coming to her baby shower. I can still see her face in my mind when I walk through Dorchester. First I thought it was not true; she couldn't be dead. But I saw everyone wearing pins with her face, the date she was born, and the date she died. I began to believe it was the truth. Paola Castillo died September 20, 2009.

I never thought someone would be able to kill a girl like Paola. The idea of someone holding a gun to her face makes me wish there would be no more pain. That's how much my heart hurt from seeing her dead.

THE KING WITH US

ANTHONY ECCLES, AGE 17

I am very tired as I leave my house on a cold Saturday morning. My tiredness meets the winter chill and they have a bad altercation. I get agitated but continue to walk. *Not that long of a walk, I'll be back in no time*, I say to myself with a smile.

As the thought lingers, I get halfway down my street and I happen to look to my left and see Martin Luther King, Jr. and his famous smile looking right at me and my not-so-famous smirk. It is pretty funny how he catches me in a smile while he's doing the same. He might just know exactly what I was thinking about. Yeah, that would make sense.

I am only going to the corner store to get some milk, eggs, and coffee cream for Mom. The second I get home I'll be able to go right back to bed. Then, I wonder, *Why is this picture facing me anyway?* It is faced towards the outside, and that has to mean something for the person who put it there. Probably an old black man living there put that picture up for other blacks like me, or for everyone to see.

PHOTO BY SHAKAYLA VENABLE

BASKETBALL GAMES ARE SWEET

JEFFREY MARTINEZ, AGE 18

When he's not playing ball, he feels like hitting someone in the face. Basketball is what makes his life sweet. So he tells people to back off just by looking at them with his red hot, spicy eyes. When he's not playing ball, he feels like eating as fast as a dog that has not eaten for five days—the same way his cousin Danny likes to eat. When he's not playing ball, he becomes Jimmy, the weapons man from *Call of Duty*.

When he is playing ball, he feels powerful. Powerful like the sun and the moon; the sun brings people out and the moon brings people inside. Powerful like air around the world that makes him live every day. Powerful like the sky.

A TRIP ON THE ORANGE LINE

ANTOINE BROTHERS, AGE 16

On the train, two friends from Greater Egleston High School are coming from Stonybrook. They are impatient because it's taking a long time to get downtown. They are seventeen and have known each other since fifth grade, when they became best friends. It's starting to get cloudy above them, but they can still see the city from a distance. Graffiti that looks freshly made with black marker covers the train's windows; it's pretty dumb, no skill.

Looking out of the side windows, they see other people across the tracks where the commuter rail runs. The next stop is Jackson Square; eleven more stops. They arrive at Chinatown, which is their favorite stop because there's a lot of diversity in the crowd. They start pacing back and forth in the car because it is taking a while to get to their destination. They can't wait to see the Celtics game at the Banknorth Garden.

PHOTO BY CHNIA WILLIAMS

As they arrive at Downtown Crossing, they are excited to get off the train and begin their walk to North Station. They have been planning to see the game for a week. Even though their tickets are for the balcony, it is just good to get out of the house.

FOLLOW MY LEAD

GEORGE RUFFIN, AGE 17

As I lead with pride and tears drift from my eyes I shout we are a family we are a team that can't be broken in between here and there — we stand today with our lives on the line to make changes not just for us but also for other folks down the line — we came too far to be looking back hold your shoulders high and grip your straps — marching up rough roads and cutting down these streets our bodies striving for something to eat — so many things we have to spot because if not we will get knocked and that would be a big loss for the ones who fought hard walking hundreds of miles — I yell keep up before you get lost stand for something or you'll fall for anything — as night falls that's when we start to creep day time's over boys ain't no time to sleep — as we get in position the faster our hearts beat every second that passes the quicker we dig in our heels and move fast — setting the horses free searching for their stash our traveling time has now passed — load up fellows

PHOTO BY GEORGE RUFFIN

quick move fast — we are squad deep with rage I command aim and shoot — guns spark with a flash end loud with a boom blast bodies dropping quicker than flies as we are stunned by our vision of such a surprise — the longer we listen we begin to move wise.

WHERE I AM FROM

CRYSELLE HENDY, AGE 18

I am from the foggy and drizzly village of devotion,

among captivating Venus Flytraps.

I am from the little country called Trinidad

where my grandma cooks callaloo, rice, stew fish,
    and coo coo.

I am from an endless ocean of a spiritual promised land,

from my great grandmother Malafy's uncontrollable constitution.

I am from the powerful and strong, the carnal and spiritual.

I am from my wisdom, knowledge, and understanding.

I learned that tomorrow is never promised,
    but the word of God can be.

I am from the Ark of the Covenant Spiritual Baptist Church

where the Christians are artificial. Many pretend to

be something they are not.

I am from a place where the sun is blistering,

from a place where the rain will never stop.

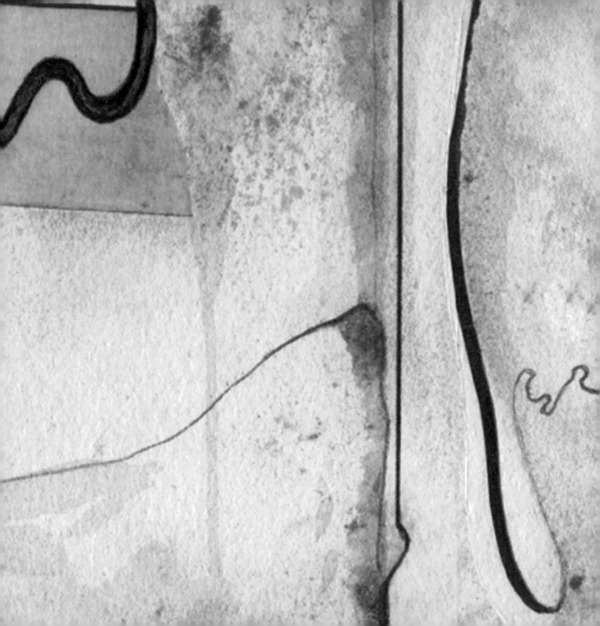

I'VE BECOME ART

WINDOW

RASLYN RICHARDSON, AGE 19

Looking out my window, I can feel the winter breeze. The day seems so long as the hours keep passing. As I look out my window, an old man catches my eye. He is tall, dark-skinned, and wears a red shirt and jeans that are ripped with holes. He doesn't have shoes and his socks are brown like mud. He has no coat to protect him from the cold. I can see the pain in his face as the wind moves him. I feel bad for the man as I look through my window.

I think to myself, *Why does he look like that? Could he have lost his job? Did his house burn down?* I put myself in his shoes. Now he is the one looking through the window. I bet he would say, "Look at that poor black girl. No home and ripped clothes." He would probably close his window from the shame of how low

PHOTO BY KENYA EDWARDS

a human being can be. Now, looking back through my window, I think about how the economy doesn't help its people: gas prices going up, health insurance too expensive. I stop wondering and ask myself a question, *What can I do to change the view through my window?*

THIS GIRL

JESSICA FELICIANO, AGE 17 ·

I hated how I had to sell drugs I hated how my mom always had a black eye I hated how I never came home to see something new in my house I hated that my friend had more clothes than me I hated how I never thought I was going to make it I hated that I was poor I hated that my shoes didn't fit I hated the stress I hated how I thought things would never get better I hated that I dropped out of school I hated that I was not that smart I hated that you would ask me how to spell a word and walk away I hated how my sister was never there for me I hated that my father didn't see me as his little girl anymore I hated how I woke up hurt every morning I hated that my mom would say he's right and I am wrong I hated that Amilea was not there anymore She's with god now but why not me?

I love how I am stronger after getting my heart broken I love how I keep myself up I love how dancing is my dream I love how my mom gave up her dream for my family I love how my dad will never be a father because I love how I made it without him I love how you make me feel I love how you always see me smiling I love how my shoes fit I love how when I am with you my heart skips a beat I love how things can't get any better I love how my mom's still here through all these things I love how my brother looks up to me I love

PHOTO BY JESSICA FELICIANO

PHOTO BY AIXA LARA

MEMORIAL

AIXA LARA, AGE 17

y background holds nothing but blue. I am crystal clear. You can see right through me. I am a memory of each and every soul that passed and their struggle to save themselves. I stand tall to show the strength each and every one of us carries. I stand strong to represent the people who are gone. I define endurance. I stand up from the middle of this busy town. People see me and they know I am the memory of many lives. Everyone who walks by can't help but stop as I stand there quietly. Walk your way straight up into my sky.

PHOTO BY RAHIYM MERVIN

THE CITY

JEAN CARLOS PEÑA, AGE 19

Oh, skyscraper! As I gaze at you,
  I can't say I admire your foundation.

Your steel has a false strength.

Your glassy exterior is astounding to the naked eye.
  I turn to the other side

& oh, city projects!

Your asphalt is stained, filthy.

Your inhabitants are always trying

to climb the established barrier.

Constantly foolish,

chasing,

never achieving,

rarely succeeding.

Though your bricks are strong,

your demise is inevitable.

I don't admire either of you,

nor am I judging either side.

I am acknowledging your existence.

I'm caught in between, wishing there was an escape.
    I wonder, *Where is the door?*

I try to walk past you but I constantly catch you from
    the corner of my eyes,

like a rude awakening.

Oh, skies!

Sculpted out of the Lord's fingertips,
  constantly looking down, you hold mysteries.

Your Creator is my guide.

Lead me to where you're going, oh Creator!
  You never had a beginning, will never have an end.

Will I ever know your thoughts?

As of now,

my exit is you.

REPRESENT

SUDAN MA, AGE 21

rowing up in Charlestown, Massachusetts was difficult. The white kids would yell, "Go pick cans out of the trash!" or, "Go read the dictionary!" I had trouble making friends with kids who weren't Asian because the community was segregated.

In the summer of 2007, the Charles Newtown Co-op held an event for residents at the housing complex. Nurses from Massachusetts General Hospital came to deliver aid kits for the community. The Asian residents were in the front of the line when a board member said, "Tell the Asians to get the hell out!" Another said, "The Chinese are everywhere. Of course, they want the free stuff. Someone tell these chinks to get out!" The board

PHOTO BY SHINEEKQUA WALKER

members were unaware that we could understand everything they were saying.

In the beginning of October 2007, I became motivated to help my community. Not just the Asian community, but everyone, so we could understand each other better. I was hired as a youth mentor at the Charles Newtown Community Center. I ran programs for the residents to bring everyone together. I wanted to show the whites that Asians do more than stay at home, read the dictionary, or pick up cans. All residents, white, Asian, Hispanic, and black, attended these programs and everyone seemed to get along. I was bringing the community together.

The day I ran for the board of directors at the co-op, I was eighteen years old and still in high school. It was intimidating for me because I ran against two older men. One man came up to me and said, "You don't have a chance on the board. You're too young and you will never understand the by-laws." The other man agreed, but I did not let their words discourage me. They only made me work harder. Each day I would go door-to-door and campaign. I was motivated and wanted my voice to be heard.

When the news broke that I had won one of the seats on the board, the man who lost complained to the residents. "It must have been a mistake," he said. "Let's recount the votes." But I had received 180 out of 263, and it was clear to everybody that I'd won. Now, I'm in a position to make a change in my community and to help others. I have to represent everybody—not just my own group. I have learned to use my voice to make sure that everyone is treated fairly.

STRONG SHOULD HAVE BEEN HER NAME

SHANESE SIMMONS, AGE 19

She has been riding this long road

looking to reveal her happiness.

Shy should have been

her name.

She uses mascara to cover

her tears.

The memories make

the black mascara

run down her

cheeks.

Emotional should have been
her name.

Although she is
  heartbroken,
she keeps a smile
  on her face.
She keeps to herself,
and thinks to herself
that she is afraid of
falling back in love,
not skipping back
to the past.

Run to the future
and see what it holds.
Strong should have been
her name.

PHOTO BY SHANESE SIMMONS

I AM

CRYSELLE HENDY, AGE 18

I am an impetuous girl who is sensitive.

I wonder what my life will be like after
I have this baby.

I see a lot of destructive things in my life
that make it harder.

I want God to save me from my enemies and
from harmful things in this world.

I am an impetuous girl who is sensitive.

I pretend to be someone that I'm not.

I feel disgusted with my impetuous self.

PHOTO BY AIXA LARA

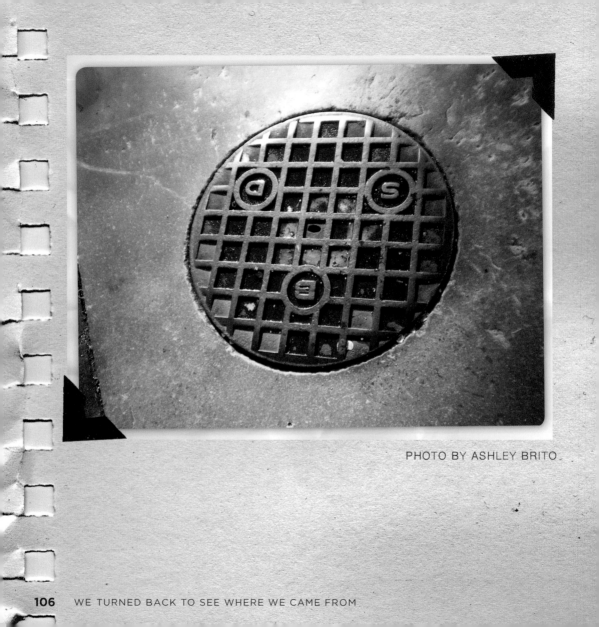

PHOTO BY ASHLEY BRITO

LOOKING FOR A NEW BEGINNING

GENESIS ABREU, AGE 19

I used to hide my issues in the old brown chest in the basement. These things took up my time and made my loved ones suffer. Over time, they made me feel like I was falling in a deep and humid sewer that smelled like decaying tomatoes. I covered my eyes in guilt because of all the bad things I had done. Being in there was scary.

When I got to the bottom of the sewer, I fell face first and floated in that stinky mud of my thoughts. I looked up and there was no way out. I caught a blurry light moving at the bottom of the thick water. Even though I came in through the top, from the darkness, it was clear from the light that I could only move deeper towards the bottom to get out.

I didn't think twice. I swam toward the little dot. I squeezed my eyes and stopped breathing for so long that the only thing I could hear was my own self, begging to escape. As I swam I became exhausted. I could hardly use my limbs to move faster, but I still got to the end. *UFFFF!! I did it, I got through!*

I thought, *Where am I? Is this a little pond? Could it be?* The sun made my eyes blurry with its brightness and I heard frogs chirping in clear water. I was pretty sure that I was in a quiet, safe place. Wait a minute! A frog's lily pad was still on my head. It reminded me that I was still forgetting something: I wanted to make amends with all the people I had hurt.

I ran as fast as I could all the way to my home. When I got up the stairs, the first person I saw was my mommy.

She said, "Little monkey, on what tree were you hanging that I couldn't see?"

Then I said, "Oh! Mommy, I'm sorry. I rested my eyes just for a minute and you wouldn't believe what I dreamed!"

She said, "Oh, Genesis! Get inside and while you're telling me, help me prepare the supper." I was so excited to tell my mother what I had dreamed, but at the same time I was thinking, *What was the meaning of it all?* What about you, the one outside my story? What does it mean to you?

FALL

GINA PEGUERO, AGE 20

s I walk, I look at the trees. Leaves fall slowly to the ground, filling the streets and sidewalks. I am allergic to the asters blowing in the air, but I still like to pick those soft and plush blossoms. I think of my childhood, when I used to blow them on my friends, and I feel like a little girl again.

On this warm day in the beginning of October, I like to go out with my friends. When I walk from school, I smell the Spanish food as I pass by a restaurant. It opens up my stomach and makes me hungry.

I wish I could be in bed, warm and wrapped in my soft grey comforter, watching movies and eating, instead of being outside. I look forward to spending time with my little brothers—playing video games, reading, and tickling them. But I'm still out in the cold.

PHOTO BY GINA PEGUERO

When I finally arrive home, I instantly take off my jacket and shoes, and take a hot shower to be fresh and warm. Being in my apartment makes me feel like I'm back home in the Dominican Republic, because it's as hot as the tropics. After getting comfortable and out of the cold weather, I feel like sitting down and relaxing my feet.

THE VALUE OF EDUCATION IS YOUR FUTURE

YASHIRA COLON, AGE 17

'd been thinking about it for months. In January 2009, I did it. I walked out of school, knowing I wasn't coming back. I was feeling depressed about my life; nothing seemed to be worth doing. I felt like my life was coming down around me as I got kicked out of my family's place. For me, school was boring, and my brothers had already dropped out.

I thought that if I dropped out of high school, my life would be easier. I wouldn't have to wake up early or do school work, which would give me a lot of free time to hang out with other friends who had also made the choice to quit school. Months went by, and I felt my life going down the drain while I did nothing. I felt like I was walking into a place with no open doors, with no future—a passage with no light, just lots of trees and ground to walk on. I realized this wasn't me. I'm an educated, open-minded girl who belongs in school.

Then one day a door opened. I saw a way to escape and make myself a better person. I thought about my dream of becoming a nurse and my new opportunity, and I didn't think twice. On October 2, 2009, I walked through Greater Egleston's doors. Everything started to change. I realized I no longer saw myself in the future I was wrongly choosing. Everything in my life is what I make it. I want to succeed. And I will.

WAITING

CHNIA WILLIAMS, AGE 17

I can't tell you how long I've been here. Freezing winters and flaming summers go by. I've been here so long. Kids walk by every day and I see them grow from miniature to large. Couples and families move in and out of the house next door. I have seen comets pass by and stars flickering. I have even seen an eclipse. Vines press into my skin and spiders crawl all over me. I've become nature. All the things I cared about before don't mean anything anymore. Makeup and clothes aren't important. I may have dirt all over me and leaves in my hair, but I've never felt this pretty before. I've become art.

TEENAGERS LOOKING THROUGH THE LENS

Where do we come from? We, the students of Greater Egleston High School, are from different countries: the Dominican Republic, Portugal, Puerto Rico, Trinidad, the United States, Costa Rica, and many other places. We all turned to Greater Egleston High School because we didn't do so well in other schools, but we all want to graduate. We are proud of the friendly teachers and thriving students at Greater Egleston. We all believe education is key to success.

Starting in October 2009, volunteers, teachers, and guest photographers from 826 Boston, MassArt, and *The Boston Globe* visited our classroom and we started to take pictures and write. We took cameras home, both digital and disposable, to photograph our community. We took photo shoot field trips to old Franklin Park, the State House, the Central Burial Ground, and the Holocaust Memorial. At first, our class didn't think this project was important, until we started taking photos and it became adventurous. Choosing angles and making images, we felt like professional photographers.

We took more than 2,000 photos altogether. Then each student picked five of his or her best photos to write about. We wrote poems, short stories, and essays about self, family, and community for one long month. After that, we started editing with staff and volunteers from 826 Boston. Later, twenty students attended a writing boot camp, where we wrote even more. After nine meetings of the student/volunteer editorial board, we agreed on a title, themes, and chapters.

We all learned how to take photos from different ranges and perspectives. But more importantly, we learned about writing, editing, and having high expectations for ourselves to complete this book. *We Turned Back to See Where We Came From* is a train moving forward while we, the passengers, look back and learn from the past. We want everyone who reads this book to know that even though we grew up in different places, we all have a lot in common. We look through the same lens but see our community differently.

Shanese Simmons

THE STUDENT EDITORIAL BOARD

Genesis Abreu	Raslyn Richardson	Shakayla Venable
Ashley Brito	George Ruffin	Chnia Williams
Jessenia Nuñez	Shanese Simmons	Shonda Williams
Gina Peguero		

To the Analysis, Writing, and
Digital Photography students,

We are pleased to have traveled with
you on your journey to becoming
published authors! You have worked hard
to successfully complete Greater Egleston
High School's first-ever published book.
The book, complete with your original photographs and writing, is a
reflection of your hard work and dedication.

    We especially enjoyed the walking field trips where we explored
our local community and downtown Boston. Traveling outside of the
classroom provided us with the opportunity to see you from a new
perspective. The images you captured spotlight your creative genius.
We are also impressed with the mature way you conducted your-
selves. You have much to be proud of.

    As your teachers, we are excited to have shared in this
momentous endeavor with you, and we congratulate you for making
history at Greater Egleston.

Kenya Edwards & Jackie Washington
TEACHERS, GREATER EGLESTON HIGH SCHOOL

ABOUT THE AUTHORS

 GENESIS ABREU, 19, aspires to become her own boss by being the CEO of a company someday. The most important person in her life is her mother.

KELMAR BRADFORD is an 18-year-old student artist from Nicaragua. He aspires to become a licensed barber and travel to Brazil. He is excited to graduate from high school this spring and begin college.

 ASHLEY BRITO, 17, grew up in the Dominican Republic. She hopes to finish school and to be a police officer or a nurse some day. The accomplishment she's most proud of is being part of this project.

ANTOINE BROTHERS, 16, is a positive person. He wants to become successful in the music industry and live in a beautiful place. His biggest success has been staying in school.

JAVIER "JACOB" CASADO, 18, enjoys taking pictures of everything. His mother and his little sister are the most important women in his life. When Jacob graduates from high school, he hopes to open his own barbershop.

 YASHIRA COLON, 17, wants to be a labor and delivery nurse because she loves babies and wants to help welcome them into the world. In her free time, she writes poems.

ANTHONY ECCLES, 17, wants to leave a positive legacy on this earth. He wants to finish high school and go to college to play football and perhaps become a lawyer. He has a very supportive mother who keeps his head on straight.

 JESSICA FELICIANO feels that the greatest accomplishments of her life so far are living to see the age of 17 and staying in high school. After she graduates, Jessica wants to become a police officer.

WILFRED GONZALEZ lives by the saying, "If you stand for nothing, you fall for everything." He is an 18-year-old Bostonian. If he could travel in time, he would go back to the past and stop every bullet that hit his friends.

CRYSELLE HENDY, 18, aspires to become a crime scene investigator. After high school, she intends to join the Marines. She loves to explore and is very proud to have come this far in her education.

AIXA LARA, 17, became successful when she was 11 years old and won a $5,000 scholarship from the Red Sox. She hopes to become a doctor and have a healthy family. In her free time, she likes to read.

 SUDAN MA, 21, was born in the Canton province of China. She aspires to become a psychiatrist or a social worker for young teens. In her free time, she tutors local students at her community center.

JEFFREY MARTINEZ is 18 years old and a Massachusetts native. Jeffrey is excited to have his work published and is thankful to his mother, the most important person in his life.

 RAHIYM MERVIN is 17 years old. When he looks in the mirror, he sees a young man who's trying to make it far in life. When this book is published, he plans to share it with his friends.

JESSENIA NUÑEZ, 18, aspires to become an event planner. She dislikes animals, but enjoys traveling and trying new foods. Someday, she would like to write a memoir.

GINA PEGUERO is a warm, intelligent 20-year-old. The most important successes Gina's had in life so far are publishing this book and trying to finish high school. She plans to be the first one in her family to go to college.

JEAN CARLOS PEÑA is a 19-year-old Dominican who has continued studying in high school despite a difficult educational journey. In his free time, he likes to read. He wants to become an artist.

AIMEE PEREZ, 17, loves children, and she cares about children with cancer even more. Someday she would like to find the cure for cancer, which is why she wants to pursue a career as an oncologist. Her mother, who is an EMT, inspires her to help people.

"I want to take care of my family," says ALFRED PHILLIPS, 17. If he could have one wish, he would want to become successful enough to not worry about money.

RASLYN RICHARDSON is a 19-year-old student from St. Croix. She believes an adage that her mother says all the time: "When you give, you will always receive."

GEORGE RUFFIN's greatest accomplishment was realizing the importance of school and changing his path. At 17, he says there are many important people in his life, but God is the captain of his yacht.

JOSHUA SANTOS, 19, is a young man from Boston. The gifts of love, friendship, family, and life are his personal foundation. He aspires to become an artist and plans to attend college.

CORENNE SKEEN, 18, aspires to become an artist. After high school, she plans to attend college. The accomplishment Corenne is most proud of is staying in school. In her free time, she likes to read.

SHANESE SIMMONS, 19, has high expectations for herself, including going to college and becoming an actress. She has many positive people telling her she can make it anywhere she wants, especially her mom, who taught her secrets and dreams she will always cherish.

SHAKAYLA VENABLE, 17, wants to be successful, finish school, and then perform forensic science and make her family proud. Shakayla thought she would never make it this far, but all her effort has been rewarded.

SHINEEKQUA WALKER is an 18-year-old student. The most important person in her life is her great grandma, because no matter what happens, she knows she can always count on her.

SHAWN WEEKS, 18, was born in Framingham but raised in Boston. He is half Puerto Rican and half black. In his spare time, he likes to write lyrics and listen to music. When he finishes high school, he plans on going to nursing school to help those in need.

MICHAYE WEST, 19, aspires to become a fashion designer. She hopes to attend the Massachusetts College of Art and Design after graduating from high school. In her free time, Michaye writes to express her feelings.

INDIGO WILKERSON, 18, wants to move to Alabama, where she will study medicine. The most important people in her life are her mother and her father, because without them she wouldn't be the person she is today.

CHNIA WILLIAMS, 17, wants to be an actress. The biggest success she's had in her life is helping to direct a play. She enjoys taking pictures of unusual objects.

SHONDA WILLIAMS, 17, was born in Boston, and hopes to earn a college degree, to pursue her dreams as an artist, and to have a better life for her family. She sees herself as a happy, strong, independent young lady with a lot of talent.

THIRTY 826 BOSTON VOLUNTEERS DEDICATED
OVER THREE HUNDRED HOURS TO THIS
SEVEN-MONTH PUBLISHING PROJECT. INSPIRED
BY THE EGLESTON STUDENTS, OUR VOLUNTEERS
ALSO SHOT PHOTOGRAPHS AND CRAFTED THEIR
OWN CREATIVE WORKS. IN THE PAGES
THAT FOLLOW, YOU'LL FIND THREE PIECES
OF WRITING COMPOSED BY 826 VOLUNTEERS
IN RESPONSE TO THE STUDENTS AND
THEIR PHOTOGRAPHS.

THIS IS HOW WE WALK

SIMONE BUI, 826 VOLUNTEER

One of us punched a hole in the wall. And the rest of us reached up, took hold of the fractures, and split the darkness open. Rocks fell like rain, and the stony cave that had trapped us dropped to its knees and crumbled at our feet. The sudden heat of the sun stung like needles on the pores of our skin, weaving a soft but feverish thread through our bones, and binding us together in fear and in hope. Warm winds streamed past our cheeks, not quite touching our faces, rushing to something beautiful and mighty a hundred miles away at the corner where three right angles collided, forging the strongest place on earth.

Lost, but liberated, we followed.

A square sheet of blue sky trailed above us, an untethered kite pushing against the stratosphere. Saffron deserts turned into verdant fields that bled into hills of poppies rising up to limestone monoliths, which flattened into prairies before melting back to desert. Enchanted, we wanted to forget the chronic darkness that came before. We wanted to make yesterday history, to follow those hurried winds to that impenetrable place where dreams don't lie face down, motionless, or go pale under the weight of time.

But when we arrived, we saw them building a grand cavern on top of that mighty corner of perfect geometry. "It's indestructible!" they hollered when they saw us coming. We stopped walking. The steel tips of our hearts dissolved into sand and the slightest breeze sifted through them.

We turned and looked back, to see where we came from, and we waited.

PHOTO BY SIMONE BUI

FLAG

JAIME ZUCKERMAN, 826 VOLUNTEER

Vines, Veins. Reaching over brick (or is it muscle?) to cover a surface long ago abandoned. That surface, cold in the cold air, is more human than one would think. Its history, the handiwork, the care, and the lives that existed there, have faded. There was a man in a white shirt who pushed carts during the day, ate spaghetti at night. There was an apartment that had a small fire on the stovetop once, which left a black smudge on the ceiling. There was a young girl who wanted to become a dancer when she was ten and instead became a store manager and a mother. There was a family that lost their mother to breast cancer, and there was a Vietnamese man who learned to speak English from a high school student at the local community center. There were families with dark brown skin and families that met on the steps at the door to talk on hot days. The building breathes. Our collective past flows through its veins. Vines. There is a faint pulse there.

PHOTO BY CHNIA WILLIAMS

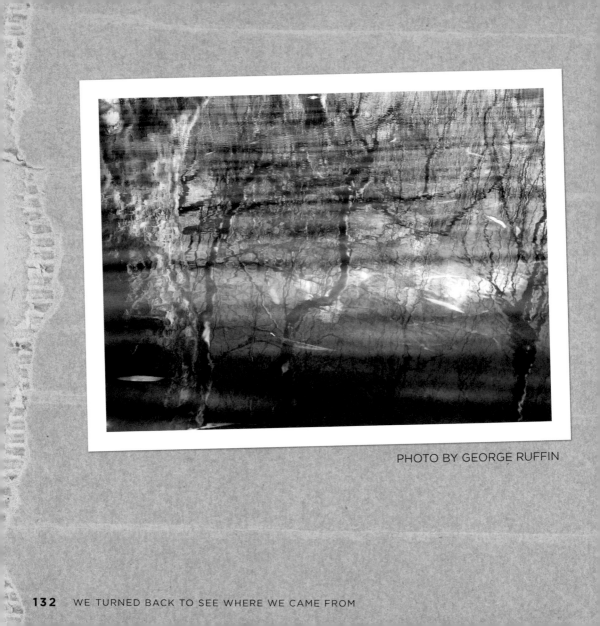

PHOTO BY GEORGE RUFFIN

PANTHEISM

BENJAMIN SUGAR, 826 VOLUNTEER

All roads lead to one.
That is our destiny.
You will see.

It's not a matter of if,
just how long we must
   sing that song.
For although hate first
   erodes from within,
eventually it will
   consume even itself.

And on that day,
when the bow string breaks,
you will see the signs,
know their meaning.
The truth,
hidden

in plain sight:
that in our dreams
we play all the characters
and in our nightmares too.

Children of the ineffable:
may we always learn,
be kind, and be generous.
Go straight to don't know.

Never forgetting what Zoltar
   once spoke
on that Venice Beach boardwalk:
one candle lights another
without ever losing any light
   of its own.

ACKNOWLEDGEMENTS

STUDENT EDITORIAL BOARD:

GENESIS ABREU

ASHLEY BRITO

GINA PEGUERO

RASLYN RICHARDSON

GEORGE RUFFIN

SHANESE SIMMONS

SHAKAYLA VENABLE

CHNIA WILLIAMS

SHONDA WILLIAMS

VOLUNTEER EDITORIAL BOARD:

BRANDON ABBS

SIMONE BUI

AMY COLLIER

ANASTASIYA DARIAVACH

DAHLIA EL-SHAFEI

BENJAMIN SUGAR

JAIME ZUCKERMAN

826 BOSTON STAFF:

DANIEL JOHNSON

LINDSEY PLAIT JONES

KAREN SAMA

MAYA SHUGART

RYAN SMITH

PROJECT LEADER:

LINDSEY PLAIT JONES

826 BOSTON BOARD OF DIRECTORS:

EVELYN ARAÑA ORTIZ

JOHN BIBLE

JON FULLERTON

JOHN GIORDANO

CAROL GREENWALD

HELEN JACOBSON

WENDY STROTHMAN

JUSTINE ROBERTS

KEVIN WHALEN

ANDREW H. COHN
LEGAL COUNSEL

**826 BOSTON
2009-2010 INTERNS:**

JOHN CAMPBELL
ELEANOR CHANDLER
NICK DECOULOS
ALYSSA FRY
MICHAEL HOLT
LAUREN MOUNCE
CHRISSY MYSKO
ASHLEY PITTS
ALICENNE REID
ANNA HALE WOLFE-PAULY

GUEST TEACHERS:
MATT LEE
SANDY WEISMAN

**826 BOSTON/GREATER EGLESTON
PROJECT VOLUNTEERS:**

AMANDA BARRETT
MIA BRUCH
SIMONE BUI
AMY COLLIER
SIRI COLOM
ANASTASIYA DARIAVACH
LAUREN DELLAQUILA
DAHLIA EL-SHAFEI
KATE FLAIM
BARBARA HAKIM
KRISTEN HOGGATT
TIM HOUSE
TRAVIS HYDE

EMMA JACOBS
IGNACIO LAGUARDA
DANIELLE MARTIN
ANNA MUDD
ANNE MURPHY
ANJULI NETRAM
ALLISON PFERSICH
JESSICA SCRANTON
JULIE SCOURFIELD
MACDUFF STEWART
JOSEPH STEELE
BENJAMIN SUGAR
DAN TURNBULL
JAIME ZUCKERMAN

826 BOSTON IS A NONPROFIT ORGANIZATION DEDICATED TO TEACHING CREATIVE AND EXPOSITORY WRITING TO STUDENTS AGES 6-18, AND TO HELPING TEACHERS INSPIRE THEIR STUDENTS TO WRITE.

OUR SERVICES ARE STRUCTURED AROUND THE UNDERSTANDING THAT GREAT LEAPS IN LEARNING CAN HAPPEN WITH ONE-ON-ONE ATTENTION AND THAT STRONG WRITING SKILLS ARE FUNDAMENTAL TO FUTURE SUCCESS. WITH THIS UNDERSTANDING IN MIND, WE PROVIDE AFTER-SCHOOL TUTORING, FIELD TRIPS, CREATIVE WRITING WORKSHOPS, IN-SCHOOL TUTORING, HELP FOR ENGLISH LANGUAGE LEARNERS, AND STUDENT PUBLICATION OPPORTUNITIES.

ALL OF OUR FREE PROGRAMS SEEK TO STRENGTHEN EACH STUDENT'S POWER TO EXPRESS IDEAS EFFECTIVELY, CREATIVELY, CONFIDENTLY, AND IN HIS OR HER INDIVIDUAL VOICE.

826 BOSTON HAS REACHED MORE THAN 3,000 STUDENTS WITH ITS FREE PROGRAMS AND OFFERED OVER 20,000 HOURS OF ONE-ON-ONE TUTORING AND WRITING SUPPORT. ADDITIONALLY, 826 BOSTON HAS PUBLISHED STUDENT WRITING IN THE *BOSTON GLOBE*, *THE NEW YORK TIMES*, AND IN A NUMBER OF ITS OWN PUBLICATIONS SUCH AS *2% OF 2% OF ALL THE WORLD'S STORIES* AND *I WISH THEY WOULD HAVE ASKED ME*.

826 BOSTON
3035 WASHINGTON ST.
ROXBURY, MA 02119
WWW.826BOSTON.ORG
INFO@826BOSTON.ORG
617-442-5400

DANIEL JOHNSON
EXECUTIVE DIRECTOR

LINDSEY PLAIT JONES
PROGRAM DIRECTOR

KAREN SAMA
PROGRAM COORDINATOR

MAYA SHUGART
VOLUNTEER COORDINATOR

RYAN SMITH
STORE & EVENTS COORDINATOR